REALITIES IN VERSE: POETIC REFLECTIONS ON THE HUMAN EXPERIENCE

SATYAM RANJAN

Made with ♥ on the Notion Press Platform
www.notionpress.com

This book is dedicated to all the dreamers, the fighters, the ones who dare to believe that they can make a difference. To those who have loved and lost, and to those who keep searching for love. To those who have struggled and fallen, and to those who have risen again. To the broken and the whole, to the ones who are still searching for their purpose, this book is for you. May these poems resonate with you, and may they remind you that you are not alone in this journey called life.

“"In 'Realities in Verse', Satyam Ranjan's poetry peels back the layers of the human experience, revealing raw truths and universal emotions"”

Contents

Foreword

In the pages of **"Realities in Verse"**, Satyam Ranjan invites readers on a journey through the human experience. Through powerful and evocative poetry, Satyam explores themes of love, loss, and the search for meaning in a rapidly changing world. These poems offer a stark and honest look at the complexities of the human condition, and they are a reflection of the author's unique perspective on the world and its inhabitants.

Satyam's poetry is a reminder that we are all connected by our shared experiences, our struggles and our triumphs. His words have the ability to resonate with readers on a deep level, and they provide a sense of comfort and understanding in times of uncertainty.

As you read through this collection of poems, you will be taken on a journey through the ups and downs of life. You will laugh, you will cry, and you will relate to the emotions that are expressed in these pages. The author's use of language is masterful, and his imagery is both striking and evocative.

In a world that can often feel overwhelming and chaotic, the poetry of **Satyam Ranjan** provides a sense of solace and understanding. It reminds us that we are not alone in our struggles, and that there is beauty to be found in even the darkest of moments. I highly recommend "Realities in Verse" to anyone looking for a deeper understanding of themselves and the world around them.

Satyam Ranjan

Preface

“"Poetry is the language of the soul, it speaks to us in a way that nothing else can" - Satyam Ranjan”

In "Realities in Verse", Satyam Ranjan takes us on a journey through the complexities of the human experience. Through his powerful and evocative poetry, he explores themes of love, loss, and the search for meaning in a rapidly changing world. These poems offer a stark and honest look at the realities of life, and they are a reflection of the author's unique perspective on the world and its inhabitants.

As you read through this collection, you will be struck by the author's ability to express complex emotions in a simple and relatable way. His words have the power to resonate with readers on a deep level, and they provide a sense of comfort and understanding in times of uncertainty.

Satyam Ranjan's poetry is a reminder that we are all connected by our shared experiences, our struggles and our triumphs. It reminds us that even in the darkest of times, there is still beauty to be found in the world. I highly recommend "Realities in Verse" to anyone looking for a deeper understanding of themselves and the world around them.

Satyam Ranjan

Preface

Acknowledgements

First and foremost, I want to express my deepest gratitude to all the people who have supported me throughout the creation of this book. To my family, thank you for your unwavering support, encouragement and for always believing in me. To my friends, thank you for your kind words, for being my sounding board and for being there for me through the ups and downs of this journey.

I also want to thank my editor and publisher, who helped me to turn my words into a cohesive and polished collection. Your guidance and expertise were invaluable to me.

I am also deeply grateful to all of my readers, who have supported me and my work. Your kind words, messages, and feedback have meant the world to me, and they have kept me motivated to keep writing.

Finally, I want to thank the world around us, for the inspiration and the beauty that it provides. From the natural landscapes to the human experiences, everything has influenced my poetry and helped me to create this book.

Thank you all, from the bottom of my heart.

Satyam Ranjan

Prologue

As I sit down to write this prologue, I am filled with a sense of both excitement and apprehension. This collection of poems represents a significant part of my life and my journey as a writer. It is a reflection of my thoughts, my emotions, and my experiences, and it is my hope that it will resonate with readers and provide them with a sense of understanding and connection.

These poems are a reflection of the complexities of the human experience. They explore themes of love, loss, and the search for meaning in a rapidly changing world. They are not always easy to read, but they are honest and true. I have poured my heart and soul into these words, and I hope that they will touch your hearts in the same way.

I believe that poetry is a powerful tool for self-discovery and for understanding the world around us. It has the ability to express the inexpressible and to connect us to our deepest emotions and experiences. Through these poems, I hope to provide you with a glimpse into my world and my perspective.

So, as you begin to read "Realities in Verse", I invite you to open your mind, your heart and to let the words speak to you. I hope that they will inspire you, challenge you and that they will leave a lasting impression.

Satyam Ranjan

1. Ashes of a Wounded Heart

I am but a shell of what once was,
A broken soul, a heart of glass.
Somedays are fine, somedays are vile,
Somedays my ashes scatter for miles.
No one cares, no one sees,
My heart is dying layer by layer, with each breeze.
I try to cry, but tears won't come,
For my sorrows have all become numb.
I wait for the moment I can fly,
Leave this pain, reach the sky high.
Friends and family, they don't know,
The depth of my despair, the weight I bear, so low.
I contemplate the rope and the clamp,
As a release, an escape from this damp.
Life was once fun, but now it's a game,
I played with those who needed me, now all is in vain.
Curses implanted, happiness torn apart,
Such a time has come, a heavy heart.
Good deeds turn to bad, fate so unkind,
So let me fly, let me leave this bind.

2. Healing My Broken Heart

In a world that seems so cold
I always gave my love, to young and old
But as I reached out my hand
No one was there to understand
I was always available, for everyone to call
But no one was there, to catch me when I fall
I helped others, with all my might
But no one was there, to make my wrongs right
I always thought of others, before myself
But no one seemed to notice, my silent yell
I was kind to all, with an open heart
But they slit my back, and tore me apart
My heart is broken, my spirit low
I cried and prayed, for someone to know
But as the darkness closes in
I realize, I must begin
To heal my wounds, and mend my soul
To find the strength, to make me whole
I'll keep walking, head held high
And let the light, guide me to the sky
I'll find my happiness, in my own way
And one day, love will come to stay
But until then, I'll stand tall
And give my all, to one and all

3. Echoes of a Broken Heart

Tears fall like rain
From eyes that once shone bright
A broken heart, a shattered soul
In the darkness of the night
Memories linger, like a ghost
Of all that once was true
A love that was once alive
Now nothing but a hue
The silence is deafening
As the pain cuts like a knife
Wishing for a way out
But there is none in sight
A heart that was once full
Now empty and alone
A love that was once pure
Now forever unknown
The rain continues to fall
As the tears stream down my face
A love that was once eternal
Now a forgotten grace

4. Confusion's Path

The path I walk is winding
And the road ahead unclear
My mind is filled with confusion
As I face my doubts and fear
I see the world around me
And wonder what it means
Why am I here, what is my purpose
And what does the future bring
I question all my choices
And the life that I have led
Was it the right path for me
Or a path that I should shed
I look for answers in the stars
And in the depths of my mind
But the truth is hard to find
And the answers hard to bind
The confusion lingers still
As I move forward day by day
Hoping that someday soon
I'll find my way.

5. Nature's Symphony

The wind whispers secrets
As it dances through the trees
A symphony of leaves rustling
Nature's melodies
The sky above is endless
A canvas painted blue
A reminder of the vastness
Of all that we can do
The sun sets in the west
A fiery ball of red
A daily reminder
Of the beauty that surrounds us, that we should not forget
The earth beneath our feet
Is alive and full of grace
A constant source of wonder
In this ever-changing place
So let us take a moment
To stop and look around
And find the beauty in the world
That surrounds us all around.

"It's a simple reminder to appreciate life and the nature that surrounds us"

6. Rising Above the Shadows

In the darkness of my mind
I feel so all alone
I see the shadows closing in
And fear I'll never know
The love and light I long for
Seems forever out of reach
I feel like a broken vessel
Beyond repair or teach
I feel like god is angry
And has turned his face away
Leaving me to suffer
In this endless night of gray
But I must hold on to hope
And believe that there is light
That even in my brokenness
I'll find a way to take flight
I'll rise above the shadows
And reclaim my power and grace
I'll walk towards the light again
And in it, I'll find my place

7. The Loneliness of a Casanova

Once, you were the life of the party
A heart that couldn't be tamed
You charmed and you seduced
And hearts you claimed
But now, you're all alone
In the silence of the night
The memories of love, they linger
But they don't feel quite right
You search for meaning
In the touch of a stranger
But the emptiness inside you
Still remains a danger
You wonder where it went wrong
And where you took the wrong turn
But the truth is, love is fickle
And sometimes it doesn't return
So you'll keep searching
For that spark that once was there
Hoping one day you'll find it
And love will be your repair.

8. The Illusion of Love

The night is dark and endless
As I lay here all alone
My thoughts a jumbled mess
That I cannot call my own
The memories of you
Haunt me still in my mind
I see your face everywhere
But you are never kind
I thought I knew love
But now I see it was just a game
I thought I knew what it was
But now it's just a shame
I built my castle in the sky
And now it's tumbling down
I thought that you were the one
But now you're just a clown
I'll pick up the pieces
And start again from scratch
I'll find my way to love
And I will not look back

9. A Glimmer of Hope

Sad and confused, a lonely boy
Wandering through life, without any joy
Searching for answers, in a world so vast
Feeling lost and alone, unable to grasp
The reasons for his pain, the cause of his strife
Wondering why he can't find love and a life
Worth living, worth fighting for each day
All he can do is pray and hope to find a way
But in the darkness, a glimmer of light
A spark of hope, that shines so bright
It reminds him that he's not alone
And guides him towards a future unknown
So hold on, dear boy, for things will change
Though the road may be long and filled with pain
Keep walking, keep moving, and you'll find your way
To a life filled with love and happiness, one day.

10. The End of the Journey

As I close this book of poetry
And bid farewell to all the words within
I take with me the lessons learned
And the memories that will always spin
Through the pages, I've shared my heart
My joys, my sorrows, my fears
But now it's time to move on
And welcome new adventures, new cheers
Though this book may be closed
And its pages may yellow with time
Its words will live on forever
In the rhythm and rhyme
As I turn the final page
And leave behind this chapter of my life
I know that the journey will continue
And there will be more struggles and strife
But with hope in my heart
And determination in my mind
I'll face the future with courage
And leave the past behind.

Satyam Ranjan

Satyam Ranjan is a poet and author, known for his evocative and powerful poetry that explores the complexities of the human experience. He has published multiple poetry collections, and his work has been featured in various literary magazines and anthologies. He believes that poetry is a powerful tool for self-discovery and for understanding the world around us. When he's not writing, he enjoys traveling, reading and spending time in nature. He currently resides in a small town, where he finds inspiration for his work in the everyday beauty of the world around him.

Other Books by Satyam Ranjan: Whispers of the Heart

Contact the Author: You can contact Satyam Ranjan via email at Satyamsingh2306@gmail.com

Follow the Author: You can follow Satyam Ranjan on social media platforms such as

- Twitter (Satyam_Ranjann)
- Instagram (satyam_ranjan)
- Linkedin (satyamranjan)
- Youtube (Satyam Ranjan)
- Google (Satyam Ranjan)

Thank you for reading "Realities in Verse". We hope you enjoyed the book and that it provided you with a deeper understanding of yourself and the world around you. If you did enjoy the book, please consider leaving a review on Amazon, Goodreads or any other book review site. Your support will help other readers to discover this book and the author's work.

Printed by Libri Plureos GmbH in Hamburg,
Germany